VOYAGING
NOME EMEKA PATRICK

This is a work of fiction. All names, characters, places, and incidents are a product of the author's imagination. Any resemblance to real events or persons, living or dead, is entirely coincidental.

Published by Akashic Books
©2024 Nome Emeka Patrick
ISBN: 978-1-63614-222-7

All rights reserved
Printed in China
First printing

Akashic Books
Instagram, X, Facebook: AkashicBooks
info@akashicbooks.com
www.akashicbooks.com

African Poetry Book Fund
Prairie Schooner
University of Nebraska
110 Andrews Hall
Lincoln, Nebraska 68588

TABLE OF CONTENTS

Preface by Matthew Shenoda 5

Good Dreams 9
A Midnight Storm, Outside the Wild 10
In the Front Pew of an Opera II 11
Aquagenic Pruritus 13
In Which Elegy Might Be Eulogy 14
[Is Not like Anybody Likes Grief, but Na Wetin Go Surely Come] 15
Aquagenic Pruritus II 16
un/still life with a flower & nothingness 18
The Lamb 20
The Alternate Life 21
The Spider 22
Prelude to Survival 24
God's Hands 25
Irapada 27
Horses in My Heart, Birds in My Mouth 29
In the Front Pew of an Opera 31
The Fallen Birds 32
Wetin I Must Give to Fit Lie under the Stars of Salvation? 33
The Clan 35
The Body Walks through Grief toward God 37

Acknowledgments 39

PREFACE
by Matthew Shenoda

In Nome Emeka Patrick's *Voyaging*, we find a work situated in the space of contemporary Nigerian poetry and specifically within a growing body of literature that explores the way gender and sexuality have been understood and challenged within that context. *Voyaging* begins in an alternate Eden, one immediately disturbed by the fractured world we embody and already succumbed to a fallen state. It is a space that the poet can dream a new opening into, and it is into that dream state that *Voyaging* takes us. Patrick's poems move in and out of dreams, blurring the lines between present and past, and reality and imagination, allowing the reader to witness and embody worlds made new and askew.

> In the beginning, I was human. My heart throbbed with music & my head
> heavy with headaches.
> ("Good Dreams")

Music and a head heavy with headaches become a beautiful stage for the poems that follow, poems that move through glory and terror in the world he inhabits and the world he imagines. The reader is pulled between these states of knowing and unknowing, often with a deft and engaged play with syntax. But Patrick does not pull us into a world singularly his own, encompassed only by his dreaming. Though he remains at the center of the poems, at every turn we are witness to the larger Nigerian community from which he hails, and we are treated to a steady exploration of the ways he is both connected and indebted to others. His joy and survival belong not only to him but to those who share this life *with* him. That community is lived and imagined, and the surreal and allegorical feature heavily here:

> In one story, a boy wakes up inside a flute. All his life
>
> became a rhythm, an entrance into melody. The rest of the story becomes
> a paradox.
> ("In Which Elegy Might Be Eulogy")

In Patrick's poems we often see a sharp turning, a slide into associative realities that remind us of the nonlinear ways in which we conceive the world. Imagination is at the center of Patrick's work, with a clear focus on the interiority of how we are and could be. There is a refreshingly honest interpretation of the self as an implicated body in the good and bad of the world. Patrick writes:

> I write poems where
> I am either an arrow or the body that suffers its violence.
> ("The Alternate Life")

And it is that consciousness of being one thing and simultaneously multiple things, that drives the urgency of these poems, which oscillate between what is real and imagined. But Patrick too grapples squarely with the place of a greater power, with the presence of God at every turn. He juxtaposes a negative portrayal of God with a God that seeks the speaker's fullness and happiness.

> In that
> life, my other life, I soliloquize into shells, and my God eavesdrops, laughs, advises me to be a comedian.
> ("The Alternate Life")

In lines like those we see a lightness imbedded in gravity. A lightness that is underpinned by the ease (at least intellectually) of knowing that the world is not binary, that we move between various emotions, realms, positions, and beliefs in complicated and often contradictory ways, and that ultimately, we encompass them all. Patrick revels in the slippages of the inbetween, in the comfort of knowing that being purely definitive is often counter to the human experience, and it is in that experience, that very *living* where these poems reside.

There is a yearning at the core of these poems, a series of conceits that pull at the desire of learning who the poet is and what their position in the world might be. It is in yearning that these poems feel gloriously full of breath. Patrick has chosen not to look away from the difficulties he and others in the world face, for all the externalizing factors we can name, but he remains rooted in both the Nigeria of his upbringing and a larger Black diaspora. In the vein of many of his contemporaries, the poems move formally, often in couplets, steadying the reader into a lyrical set of movements that flow seamlessly from one line to the next. There is a clear and considered manner in this work that seems consciously engaged with the works of other poets, not only with his contemporaries, like Romeo Oriogun or Ugochukwu Damian Okpara, but also with the works of poets who have influenced his work, like Carl Dennis, whom he names in "The Alternate Life."

What is perhaps most uplifting is that in the end, through a series of explorations on grief and personhood, the self and community, Patrick brings us to a place where he concedes:

> The world is beautiful.
> There are no two ways about it. The streams running to meet
>
> their one true source, their babbles. O, the world, the world

wants me
to love it. Despite its terrors, despite my errors. Lord,
whose debt am I?
("In the Front Pew of an Opera II")

GOOD DREAMS

In the beginning, there were apples on the floor where the garden could have
been a paradise were it not for the blare of a car on the other side of the walls.

In the beginning, I drew my water from a well. Not to quench my thirst for joy
but to water the garden. I imagined that if the field *is* green, I'd someday lie in

its soft tongue and dream away the ache. Outside myself, what am I but a white
calf? Around me, my future is an umbrella. Above me, my frame is a flourishing
      forest.

In the beginning, I was human. My heart throbbed with music & my head

heavy with headaches. The rainbow pills, the glass of still water & the sun glitzing
onto my bed reminded me of my mortality. I have dreamt the daisies—cut off the

branches, built boats from the remains of doubt. I know nothing of the universe's
hunger for my blood. The family nurse beats my wrist, in place of veins, I imagine

a tunnel, inside it, secrets reversed into memories. I keep prancing inside
the stillness of my sorrow, hoping to outgrow it. I am red in the language of my loss.

In my dreams, I touch myself thinking of the birds. In place of a moan, something
inside my mouth wails. I make love outside my body. I storm into the temple,

instead of pews I find pebbles from a dark past. I'm living inside
a grove, yet the vision translates it to a grave. Here, my good heart. In the beginning,

I fell past a hell and rose inside the haze of a heaven. This is my belief.
I slept inside my sadness, woke up a salvation. In my wake, God says my name.

A MIDNIGHT STORM, OUTSIDE THE WILD

The night is a wet grave. I'm in a room whose dark has eyes.
Its windows animated by the raindrops from a dark sky. Outside,
a man walks on the street with a loud stereo—his voice lilting
the night's calm. Another man walks with his daughter. Silence sits,
stirs them like a god. Let's imagine this: a lone cub suddenly finds
itself in this poem trapped in a midnight storm. Fear has a dialect.
Its vowels are heavier than thunders. Tonight, I am breathing in
and out because therapy. Because the heart has to keep its bell's ring
raw. Because the body must hold its animal from sprinting into
the wild. Once again, I am basic: human trapped in the garb of flaws.
Loneliness is a tongue beaten off its blue leap. I name two things I'm not:
a failure, a disappointment. Who says I can't be happy with all
the Lord has done for me if not grief? In life, something takes the
nape of our necks to slabs, sets a knife to it. Say death. Violence. Say loss.
Say depression, parents, teachers, and even ourselves. The lark behind my
heart's hut sings all day. It never knows when to stop. A hymn
that cliché should mean something other than *being alive*, yea? *Above* life,
I hold life—at least, it is what Jesus wants me to do. Once, in a fever
dream, I saw my grandmother's ghost eating a pear with salt.
I woke up the next morning and googled DIYs about how to eat with the dead.

IN THE FRONT PEW OF AN OPERA II
after Giuseppe Verdi, Nabucco

I have been listening for the signs behind the bat's nightmares.
I have found nothing less astonishing. I have touched

the sculptures sure that they'll be here even after I leave the earth.
Maybe in decades to come, in a house where younger versions

of me drop flowers by my feet. Old perhaps and full of the love
of the woman I desired. I do not want to leave this place, not just yet.

Even though the sky falls by layers. Even though the child
loses its way searching for the prints of God in the wild. I do not

want to leave this place. Not yet. Not with all the good souls.
The lips that have memorized mine, the strangers who have offered me

water in the dreams where I travel thirsty. The world is beautiful.
There are no two ways about it. The streams running to meet

their one true source, their babbles. O, the world, the world wants me
to love it. Despite its terrors, despite my errors. Lord, whose debt am I?

On the stage, the violinist plays all the notes. He trades his sadness
for sonatas. The conductor knows my grandmother. He has her eyes.

O, the way he moves! What is this symphony, what is this music that
speaks to my life? what stress what pause what falls

what is the magic that is this composition? Someday, when
I die, I hope this, among others, ushers me home. A song in

a language I failed to learn. The world is beautiful though I spend
most of my life sorting the capsules of happiness. Sleeping inside

the body of women whose names I may not remember in the next
decade. God, forgive me if I ever questioned too much. My doubt

ushers me closer to your altar. Closer even to the sanctuary
where I lie naked. A mat of memory. A cat seeking light after threading

the dread of darkness. Once again, I know I am God's debt.
Yet, I know the world wants me. It wants my tired heart.

AQUAGENIC PRURITUS

Dear, should I be afraid?   Long April suns. Nights
        bald of sleep—I should get my garments off
and tip it for a currency that will save me
        a rainbow of pills. Once, the chemist pricked
my skin. Took my blood but found nothing
        fatal in its focal.
God sat amid birds, modelled me into man,
        carved inside my heart a bell. To be honest,
I too am marveled, how close I was once to life.
        Now, in every song, I almost hear the liturgies of
dying. In my dreams, I am half-song, half-life and mostly
        the lifespans of half-moons. My mother calls to me
in her mother's mother's dialect. The echo
        of her voice tilts me off the hill of my life. I fall,
become an eternal eulogy. A wobble of waterfalls. My clone writes
        folktales in which I am either a sea fairy or a sailor
because it's easy to wake up and imagine the world
        folded into water again. Noah's fear. In my dreams, no
Noah, no Arks except for tilapias witnessing
        the wiggle of water. They want me to live with this
pain. To destroy the paintings. When it is time
        for me to leave, they held me by my faith.

IN WHICH ELEGY MIGHT BE EULOGY

Then, acknowledgement. Then, praise. Salvation. But, severed limbs,
the wool of an animal stuffed into the wounds, the fresh blood coughing,

a gallop of red. To alter is to manifest. A version of another. I find my names
on the temple's floor highlighted by a holy shadow. A prayer. The tongue's

loyal obsession to praise. I cut the vine, trudge the yards. I mistake
the ruins for reason. In one story, a boy wakes up inside a flute. All his life

becomes a rhythm, an entrance into melody. The rest of the story becomes
a paradox. I want a new name given my hunger. A river drunk with mercy.

All the baskets of first sons retrieved. I want a new hunger, given a name.
Peace. I just want a hymn where it should be. The red of blood, honeyed

out of my tongue. I want to open the door holding a knob, never a knife.
To sever the grief, a dagger. Then, a hole brimmed red. I wish love for

the doves standing inside the groves of my fears. O, the solitary wings
of what lies beside our futures. The white of uncertainty. How do I sacrifice

the lamb knowing God might never speak? I lie on the temple's floor.
The cold, a eulogy eating my skin. A psalm trapped in my throat, a stone,

a benediction blazing still, the chorus rising in the proximity of choruses.
Heavenly Father, use me according to your will—make me your most loyal verb.

[IS NOT LIKE ANYBODY LIKES GRIEF, BUT NA WETIN GO SURELY COME]

Sometimes, na the door. A consonant of creaks always
behind it. Other times, it is just the heart unmasking
itself behind worry's blur sacristy. A horse bothered about weather.
I'm not sure about this, but one thing na for sure: grief will always be a butchery.
Grief go always get plenti voices. It doesn't have to be anything
that has a name in my dialect or yours. The clock ticks a mantra
that'd snake its way into my nightmares. On lonely days,
when I lie down inside the fever of my own fear, I imagine
an animal inside it, the tick tock of its heart plummeting
against its body. A miracle that is not even miracle enough.
In this poem I'm a dusty bulb, but I'm already broken in like 10
other poems. Even me sef dey try piece myself together.
E get why. Is not a crime to have something to imagine na.
Say the body a flower inside a storm. Once, I spoke my
name into the eyes of a dog just mek I see how e go react.
To tell you the truth, most days, I go just siddon dey
think of the korret trails to death. Is not a crime to walk toward
something that is bigger than you na. Of all things to do,
loss sits by a man who is not my father but has my father's
smile. Can you even imagine that? A man morphed into metaphor.
Honestly, no be ordinary eye say pesin go just say e wan
shut all the doors to light. I don dey talk too much, but
there is still a whole vowel of blackbirds monothonged in my
mouth. Is not all that bad to sit inside the groves of my grief
listening and watching the birds fly by. The doves, the bats,
the songbirds. Their wings a prayer motioned toward a god.

AQUAGENIC PRURITUS II

Two of my grandmother's children died before they were 14,
                but I made it
        past 20. So death isn't hereditary after all.
The sun is a glowing bird perched on the hospital window.
        My father sits
in the visitors' space, his eyes dart,
        shift now & then
                                        toward me.
        The last time he sat to wait in a hospital,
it was to claim my mother's still body,
                robed in white, kept aside like a gift.
Maybe it was. Maybe death is a gift.
I'm not dying yet, but somehow,
                      something has brought me
to this building where corpses are wheeled into dark rooms,
where even the tick tick of my heart surprises me now.
        When the doctor asks me when it all started. That is,
when water became ants biting into my skin,
he picks a pen,
        sets to write.
        What does it mean to document the prologue
of a tragedy?
        What difference does it make where the fire starts
scraping a chapel?
            God melts my tongue into silence.
Shea butter mounted under a burning sky.

            I don't know. It just started.

Back home, I swallow medications until my tongue yellows
then reddens. Inverted by invention.
                         In the bathroom, I stand
for minutes contemplating why water would hurt anyone.
I have heard tales about drowning,
             but who blames water for gravity,
                 for the body's resistance to floating?
This poem is about water, about body, but I wanted to tell you:
        even a door could be a coffin.
The body is always canoeing toward the mercy of something
        that growls or glows.

UN/STILL LIFE WITH A FLOWER & NOTHINGNESS
Your body told me in a dream it's never been afraid of anything.
—Richard Siken

The world doesn't still as it should. Instead it sways.
In the dream, I bludgeon from myself into myself

until every catalogue of me becomes a door through which
I must snail through to become whole. A part of something

is already that thing. I pluck my hands. In place of it I search
around for a black flower, thick and beautiful, to fit

but find nothing. So, I go on with a part of me still on
the floor. It's a dream. I can't tell if I am laughing or sobbing.

Either way, I know my life has become a riddle. A story whose
jagged end I must discover before it happens. I kneel naked

inside a room. It is warm, wet, so I guess I am kneeling inside
myself. The music in the room is my heart's own beat. I hear it.

See, arrhythmia could be a lullaby, depends on whether
you're sleeping or dying. A boy can be a mystery, depends on

what animal stands at the threshold. God's eyes on its dark fur.
Depends on whether he is in the cave of a dream or outside it.

O, rift of lilting illusion, it is difficult to hymn with my tongue
tainted with apple, which means this must be Eden; difficult to

believe this is Eden because I am fully clothed, and there are
no trees. The sky isn't really a sky but a vast sheet of colorless

wet field (and inside the wet field little birds hatching into flight).
Beneath the sky, raccoons. Their tails gilded in a new glow.

As I walk, my feet, against the floor that isn't a floor but
a carpet of nothingness, ask, *What sense do all these make? What?*

I want to feel whole, so I pluck out my other arm. Listen, this is
the mystery. Inside the dream, any God would think me a flower.

THE LAMB

Truly, all I want is to empty my blood into the lamb's still heart.
First, it is the gash. A border iced into a clot, old blood mounted

at its entrance. The lamb has spent a day or two in the wet, wet
grass, rain hissing its way into its fur, a wet dirge, pulsating hymn.

Because to be dead is to become empty, the dark river of its existence
flowing off its origin. The lamb a *still*, caravan of a carcass. Its flesh

a flute where sound goes to rust. In my dream, my dead ma picks rotten
plums off a porch, wraps her lips into a monologue: asks God questions

my father belches away. The theory is grief. The body is its practice.
The lamb is a land struck by an omen. The lamb is a door widowed

off its hinges. The lamb is a museum where the dead come to sigh.
Listen, the myth is: in every mouth, there's a mole. The fact is: in every

mole, a melody glints bright like a meteor. All I want is to harbor
my heart inside the lamb's still body. A corpse translated into a clone.

In another dream, I am all the lamb ever wants. Its shield. Its shepherd.
Its avoidable slaughter and slander. For nights, the lamb lies dead at the

threshold of my dreams. Its body collating the glow of God's garment.
Nights, I slumber to warthogs racing in my blood. A pulse of thumps.

When the lamb finally heaves, it does so in my mother's dialect. It says
my name in Iyemi's voice. Inside its eyes, my dead mother's eyes swirl.

THE ALTERNATE LIFE
after Carl Dennis

I earned a degree quoting the many thoughts of Shakespeare,
Marlowe, Elliot, etc. Every night, my head bent at the reading
table where the lamp light licks my eyes into an itch, an epitaph
echoing in my mind because I thought books were going to be
the destrier that'd gallop me to my slaughter. In my other life,
I am a boy, and what do I know except to run alongside the other
boys, bare skin, leaf-pants. Our bodies wet from the river's
very spittle. I climb trees, learn the dialects of leopards, sleep
with birds cooing by my bedside. In that other life, a boy my age
who has my face slits my wrist and what gushes out is gold, and we
aren't surprised. In our lexicon, there is no word for *force, kill, bite,*
etc. The closest word to violence is forty syllables long. In my
current life, I'm an ellipsis —a thread traveling in the tendon of a
dead animal. I wake up every night amid bones clacking then
distilling into ash. In this life, I'm 23, sober, jobless, have dreams
where I stand before students who'd never hesitate to laugh at
how I pronounce their fathers' fathers' names. I write poems where
I am either an arrow or the body that suffers its violence. In that
life, my other life, I soliloquize into shells, and my God eavesdrops,
laughs, advises me to be a comedian. The angels nod, agree with
Him. I'm a bridge and a boon. I build lives out of ligaments. My clan
puts me on a camel to save a dying continent. I am neither a lamb
nor a wolf. I am a tree at a river's tongue, which means archangels
gather around me to assign duties to destinies. In my one true life,
I search for joy. Colted by loss, paddled by ghosts of women who
planted their names in my ribs before knowing the calm of coffins.
In that other life, I am no one's child, even joy begs to adopt me.

THE SPIDER

Inside the silence, I hear how light take fall before e come rise again
like a ghost to crawl around the room. The sacrament is solitude.

The shadow shifts, a loyal slave to the light, in place of the body.
The spider knits its webs, builds an empire nightly while I lie

in my own sweat thinking: *What is this life? What . . . this life?*
The spider wants my dream but doesn't understand where my sleep

becomes a haunting. This is the horn of ignorance. How long does
the animal have to stay awake to be christened? My bones a flute,

a whistling of age, ageing. My lover drops me voicemails. Inside
her voice, a child crying. How does a voice make us into a thing

far from its destination? There are many more nights before the dark
gives me back my eyes. My sleep. My good dreams. The light rises

on the wall, slumps back upon my body. My chest bare, my face
pimpled, my beards a forest at night, but my mouth a monastery

in its hour of stillness. I have been writing about God so much
that They step out of my poems, frustrated, flustered. Shey my

hands neva carry enuf of these logs? Where the promise dey for all diz
words wey I dey yarn? Would I were a book, the prologue would note

God's names or my mothers'. True and through, I sleep inside my solitude.
A bird dreaming of the sky's blue while the arrow approaches.

The bird falls, but outside the arrow's imagination. In truth, the spider wants to teach me to grow in the dark of my life, web it into language.

PRELUDE TO SURVIVAL

I am at the stage in my life where leaves floating down a tree
could mean a disaster, rather than descent. I should break

the bread and hold the chalice to the walls. Forge a communion
with everything that's tried to kill me. I should skip the ropes,

pretend my body leaping off the earth is therapy. Or wait at
the foot of the cherry tree, pretend the blades of grass waving

in the garden are ghosts of someone who loved me before I was
born. I was named a promise, altar erected in place of affection;

but what, now, is this oil spilled on the mirror? A drowning
where a face should be. My image in the mirror's lung almost

a façade. I wrote happiness in every diary and went back to find
a tooth decayed in its place, inked page smeared by the blood

of something that wasn't born but imagined. Once, I slipped
into my grandma's room to be sure she was still there. On the wall,

her shadow, its movement a memento. Some days. I am so
theater, grief audiences in me. Every *uhhs* & *ahhs* rusted pins

tipped into a balloon. Thus, I fall apart, ruins of the ruined.
I can't tell what time it is in this darkness. Blood whistling like

a sizzle. But I can feel the flowers unfurling, dawn rising to meet
dread where, if my body rises, it must be the prelude to a magic.

GOD'S HANDS

Now: the August of ache. The wound pretending not to be a wound, sunshine and shame. 23 hours, 35 minutes, and the clock still chuckling

what sounds like my name. The algorithm of my life leaping inside my breath, in and out—*tra-la-la* goes the thread. I want so much to

stick my tongue out for the honey, to taste the sweetness my birth never really promised. I want so much to christen my heart, pull it

off its cage, and plant it in a garden. This is in a dream. Inside it, paper planes find their ways into a furnace. It's too early to walk into

the fire in search of a promise. The wound widens like a yawn, closes again, wings of a sojourning egret. Inside my mouth, I'm holding a

light. A hole torched by a moon's meme. Here in my hands, I gather all the mangoes. But instead of ripeness, ruin. I want to stand here

by the door, outside the door, to peep into myself, aches and alchemy. At the door, outside the door, to swallow all of me, scars and sunsets.

I'm a lone chapel. I sit so still in the dark of myself watching a single firefly. I stake religion trying to find a good route to the self. I stand

so far from the audience, I forget what it means to be touched here, here and there. The arithmetic is grief. I trade my sleep for cheap thoughts

and afterlife fantasies. Once, I lowered my fear into my bed, imagined it was my life. The soft moans of it, its secret hisses, its daily loneliness.

The puzzle of grief lies in life. I keep hurling lamps out my window.
I imagine God's hands doing the same to my life. Laughing, of course.

IRAPADA

I have been harvesting what fruits of grief the world
planted on my fields. Now, I must cut a bit of shade from

hope and put my pickles to rest. True, the thirst of joy launches
me to the rivers, where I go on all fours, an animal clocked alive

by want, lip the water. My tongue against the water a rhapsody.
Sorry, I mistake my want for a wade. My wail for a wall. O, what

strange dialect must I speak to arrive inside my body? The larks
behind me are a temple, the voice of God rising like Lazarus from

the hollow of their beaks. I am alive, even if briefly. Even if
the script drowns in the bathtub. In bathrooms, my sponge makes

my skin into a salt. The silence of light reentering light,
a darkness we call by name until it becomes ours. Well, what'd

the universe say about my voyage into my own body? The wolves
howling to christen my shadow a god. It flies again, the myth

I keep in my bones, the dreams, the lamb of me treading toward
the pyre, where God keeps the fire burning to light the world.

True, I sleep half into myself, rummaging the other half
for the true match to the true lamp. The artist sleepwalking

into his own self-portrait. The river runs dry. Instead of sand,
I find a swamp. What would I not do to cut the apple of me

from that tree, from the garden where all animals come to face
with their own night-storms? I don't know what I would truly be

with no grief. A paper of a human, empty, until filled again by
God's own musings. Though, I have been running around the

field, a mule of my own world, I must walk back inside, pull out
a chair, pour me a glass, sit at the table, and look at the field, my grief.

HORSES IN MY HEART, BIRDS IN MY MOUTH

Almost every night uncracks the legend of an ache.
If I am good enough, I'd live to see another night. The bridge in my ribs

collapsed into a boon—living translated into levity. The truth is,
sometimes I want to hear the giggles of a child in the lightning.

A rhyme in the roar. Something we can all marvel about. I miss my
heart and I miss my heart—a calm where the horses come to rest,

a return into their regal. In one myth, a Black boy offers a beast his
tongue, its hymn and harmonies, hoping it will rewrite hunger

into homily. Some things are not to be said of hunger. Imagine how I
fit just dey make I dey get hunger for blood, to siddon in my solemn

and think of a nail driving into a palm, or the horse's head chopped off
its neck—its body a wet rattle, dying in all the soft places. Its visions

with it. No be say I want diz things. Nobody want that kind thing sef,
but it's just my heart riddled with something bigger, something dark

enough to hide its gold. I am not what they say I am. The cattle of me
labors, but what does it get in return? Lashes for a surname. To say

I sabi grief na to say I sabi my papa's papa slang—the lilt of a lineage.
I wobble my way into the dark, strapped with a crucifix of wounds.

I take to my hands the shreds of my disappointments, mispronounce
my god's sobriquets. This is not the first time I imagine the dark a lone

chapel, mistaking my shadow on the wall for an angel, wings scraped off its back. In my mouth, day-old birds shrieking in the dialect of a disaster.

IN THE FRONT PEW OF AN OPERA
after Richard Siken

    There are so many tongues to switch the songs into without
waking the cats that sleep in our hearts;
        there are many notes that begin even before the pianist's
fingers draw tunes from that black-and-white machine.
        Where are you? And how are you today?
Imagine this is April, and the sunflowers are proof enough that
        we are alive, and the cobbler across the street makes us sandals
that we might never wear. You're in the bed, you're out of bed, you're
        in the kitchen making us spag, you're sitting across the table
toasting to long life, though when you say *to long life* I imagine
        you said to *the days when I won't be here*, and you're in the bathroom
singing the walls to mirrors.
        After you left, I'd have dreams where a woman with your smile
walks out the door into a dam; on some other dream, I'm suddenly
        in a bathroom where the floor is a carpet of rubble,
on some other, I'm in an empty tub pushing my heart back to fit in
        my chest. On some days, the memory of you'd be a violence
and in others, your scent would fill my veins like blood;
        How are you? —I trudge the land of my lonely, picking stones,
mistaking them for seeds. It is planting season and the seeds haven't
        sprouted. Anything would grow but a stone. Why then
does this grief leap taller than the sunflowers in the garden?
        I'm sitting in the opera room and the songs are just shadows
tumbling out of a window. Imagine if grief can be this ordinary, this small.
        Imagine if you were here, you'd have hummed along the notes
as though a lark made a labyrinth in your throat.
        I imagine now that you were here. Even the clouds moving outside
would have been something we could laugh about,
        our voices balloons bouncing against each other, tender in the right places.

THE FALLEN BIRDS

Holy of all nights, what is this lush where I expected a lantern?
Tell me, what is this lilt, this lament, this revelation like the spleen

of a premonition stuck in a raven's chest. Believe me, I been don dey
sing outside the garden, unaware of the birds and where they tremble.

I had thought the wind a widow fluting an elegy for a child trapped
behind, not inside, not within, a darkness. O, camel of my cravings,

I walked the desert burdened by how many kilometers I must
travel to meet astonishment. What symphony, what synonym lies

beneath the hooves of my pain? I lost only to be farther to what I feared.
The horse traveling through a swamp to its origin. I want nothing

but a blessed mole, a scar where there should be one. Listen, call me
by my name even if the darkness finds me in this voyage. Call me even

when my whimper whirls louder than my want. Trust me, trust my
bones to strike the right bells. Trust the birds to flap out of their nests.

I want the keys even if the doors are diameters of a disaster.
Lord, may I find the lush. May I find the lantern. And at the end,

an altar erected in my name, a lamb, a knife, and a God
who speaks the language of broken hearts. A God who listens too.

WETIN I MUST GIVE TO FIT LIE UNDER THE STARS OF SALVATION?

I have given up the sad tale of living,
translated its lexicon
into a riddle.
The river constantly going against its exegesis.
Inside its voice, the drowning of unknown things.
Yes, I want this fall,
body whole into the ocean of this myth,
my curiosity a stone at the most lonely part
in the ocean's mouth.
Too tired to do the daily sail toward shore,
my storms grow louder,
their mood switching from archipelago to apocalypse.
I come blind to avoid the blood,
to cross the door a shadow and the light trapped
around its science. This second, what do I know
but to open my bones to the flute of salvation.
Pathway into the prolixity of prayer.
Lord, I've come but to what hut?
Tired, I sleep inside my anxiety,
arise the damp of dawns. What is it really,
what does the world want
from my temple, what old song
must I chant to sink back into rest?
What red, what black . . . what color
must my hungers have for them to be believed,
held up away from the axe?
The stone cast not into grave but glory.
I no know wetin I must give

to fit lie under the stars
of salvation: stack of nairas or a cry
tinted with the urge of an arrow.

THE CLAN

I have been asking the same questions over and over again.
I blame the metaphors, not the mirrors. I blame

my hands, not my heart. I no sabi who the pendant of pain
belong to. Na half the room, half the stage, abi na the whole

lineage? I want no answers I have already. Na we get am. It is ours.
But we don't know what to do with them. I take no offense in the blood.

The symbol reminds me again and again, how much closer
we grow toward our graves. Still, there's nothing we haven't

mourned. The salt has melted in our home countries.
Where do we return to? We rummage the ashes for names.

We search for traces of families in the bones. O, we
have mourned. We have loved. The herd traveling always

through the skyfalls, holding hands. The thunder rumbling
our children's names. The lightning, God's failed attempt

at lighting our paths. When the rain falls, it touches even our
most sacred scars. No one wakes up a haunting unless haunted.

Yet, we love. We break the kola nut open, laugh at the bonfire,
make love to our beloveds, and the world spins on, a dice spun

by angels at intervals. Wine, many cups of—we shall drink and not
mistake the red for rage, the bland for blood. Y'all, we shall walk

around the tree sure enough that our feet are feathers; prayers, promises that we are still here. Children of the world, of God.

THE BODY WALKS THROUGH GRIEF TOWARD GOD

In a dark room
where the skirl of an angel's hosanna
scurried inside the walls like the shadows of a myth,
I pulled out my heart

searched for the knoll of grief,
the paralytic mound of an ache
that widens into a dark nill.
I've been trudging the trails of my life.

On my voyage,
magpies eulogize the bedlam of my body
every other night,
I set my bed ablaze to keep my family warm.

The lie is that no one hurts,
the truth is: even the sky mourns a loss,
the boon is I am a dove nestled behind God's hands,
holy percussion.

O, what is grief if not the mortician
that travels through the body?
Sometimes, I am a dent closer to happiness,
a wolf licking the moon off the dark.

Truly I say unto you,
life whets everything,
but why are our bones this responsive to loss?

I am sorting out the apples
from the appendage.
I am cutting my Aprils off the Appendix.
That is it. That is the closest
my fingers ever came to purpose.

To be honest, there's sometimes a silence
when the sheep seeks a shepherd.
Sometimes, wail coats its body

where there should be wool.
The fact remains: a guillotine would often be an omen.
The arrow lurched into distance
would sometimes split the wrong rib.

I sabi say even awa eden fit be sabotage
and awa hands no go fit be
paddle enough for all the katakata
wey the world don heap ontop awa bodi,

but no one should come this close to healing
and watch it slip away.
Brethren, the closest my eyes came to God
was in the blur.

ACKNOWLEDGMENTS

Waxwing: "un/still life with a flower & nothingness" and "Prelude to Survival"
TriQuarterly: "[Is Not like Anybody Likes Grief, but Na Wetin Go Surely Come]"
Narrative: "Horses in My Heart, Birds in My Mouth"
Frontier Poetry: "In the Front Pew of an Opera" and "The Body Walks through Grief toward God"
WestBranch: "Wetin I Must Give to Fit Lie under the Stars of Salvation?"